Love is What Makes Us a Family

Julia E. Morrison and **Laura Knauer**

Eliza

*Diane,
Thank you for supporting all kinds of families! ♥ Julia Morrison*

*Diane -
thank you for your support!
Laura Knauer ♥*

Archway Publishing books may be ordered through booksellers or by contacting:

Archway Publishing
1663 Liberty Drive
Bloomington, IN 47403
www.archwaypublishing.com
1 (888) 242-5904

Because of the dynamic nature of the Internet, any web addresses or links contained in this book may have changed since publication and may no longer be valid. The views expressed in this work are solely those of the author and do not necessarily reflect the views of the publisher, and the publisher hereby disclaims any responsibility for them.

Any people depicted in stock imagery provided by Thinkstock are models, and such images are being used for illustrative purposes only.
Certain stock imagery © Thinkstock.

ISBN: 978-1-4808-2817-9 (sc)
ISBN: 978-1-4808-2816-2 (e)

Print information available on the last page.

Archway Publishing rev. date: 06/22/2016

For Eliza, my favorite girl in the whole world. And for all of the grownups out there who are having these important conversations with the little people in their lives.

-JEM

For Aven, whom I love more than anything. I am thankful for your patience and understanding and your sweet, happy attitude as we navigate the changes in our own family.

-LK

This book would not have been possible without the love and support of our amazing donors:

Erin Annis

Enid Axtell

Kimmy Benson

Gretchen Bradley

Melissa Brazeale

Laura Brodaczynski

Heidi Charlestream

Traci Chun

Emily Corak

Brandy Cortnik

Erin Davolt

Terri DeMaris

Liz Derrough

David Dorr

Joe and Carol Durocher

Liv Edens

Tom Ethen

Courtney Eyer

Jeanne Federovitch

Rebecca Foster-Rife

Mckayla Giesbers

Anneliese Gomez

Corina Gomez

Margaret Gomez

Kim Hansen

Chris Hayes

Phil Hays

Irene Hess

Kristina Howe

Beck Ivie

Chris Jenkins

Emily Jinnah

Kelly Johnson

Angela Jones

Meaghan Joyce

Joseph and Claudia Kotowicz

Ellen Leher

Sarah LePage

Mary Levenhagen

Josh Lucy

Jen Martinek

Jeni McAnally

Brad McKerihan

Nancy McLain

Leslie Morrison

Jane and Don Montgomery

Lynn Morrow

Carlene Ostedgaard

Laura Pettit

Tito Piliado

Trish Piliado

Sherri Priestman

Gretchen Richter

Josh Rife

Jennifer Roberts

David Rosenthal

Roy and Jane Rosenthal

Irene Sandler

Jon Selby

Lindsey Snodgrass

Pam Stanek

Jessie Stone

Stephanie and Ryan Stutesman

Zach Tautfest

Leah Thorp

Karina Tobin

Lauren Van Dyke

Elana Wendel

Ruth White

Meagan Williams

Hi! I'm Eliza. I'm six years old.

Meet my mom and dad.

We used to live in one house together,

3

but then my parents got divorced.

4

Divorce is when two grownups decide
not to be married anymore.

At first I was sad, but my mom and dad will always love me and that's what really matters most!

Now I spend half of the week with my mom, and the other half of the week with my dad. I have two houses and two beds and different toys at each house.

It took me a little while to get used to having two homes,
but each place is special to me for different reasons.

My house isn't the only thing that's changed. My dad has a girlfriend now.

9

My mom does too.

When I'm at my mom's house, the two of
us do lots of fun things together.

I like it when her girlfriend is there too.
She's nice and fun to be around.

12

When I'm at my dad's house, we spend time together.

We also have fun with his girlfriend. I like her, too.

14

Sometimes I get confused, so
I ask my parents questions.

15

"Why does mommy
kiss girls?

"Well, sometimes mommies
fall in love with mommies,
and daddies fall in love
with daddies."

16

18

"It's okay that Mommy loves girls, right?
Because girls can marry girls and boys can marry boys."
"Of course, what matters is that they love each other, and we
all love you."

"Do you still love Daddy?"

"Yes, I still love him, and I always will. I love him differently now, like a friend, but we'll always be family."

20

Talking to my mom and dad always makes me feel
better. Sometimes families change, and that's okay.
There are lots of different ways to be a family.

The most important thing is that we are happy, and we love each other. Love is what makes us a family.

Meet MY family!

Now, tell me about YOURS!

Things to talk about after reading:

1. Do you know anyone with two mommies or daddies? What do you think about that?

2. Eliza talks to her parents when she has questions about her changing family. What are some questions (about Eliza's family, or your own) that you could ask a grown-up about?

3. What makes a family? Talk about all of the things that make people a family.

4. Who is in your family? Talk about what makes each member of your family special.

5. Eliza likes to spend time with her parents. What are some fun things that you like to do with the grown-ups that you live with?

Resource page:

- **Follow the authors' blog** for additional resources and updates on future books
    - www.juliaemorrison.com

- **Family Equality Council** is changing attitudes and policies to ensure all families are respected, loved, and celebrated - especially families with parents who are lesbian, gay, bisexual, or transgender.
    - www.familyequality.org
    - Phone: (617) 502-8700

- **Gay Parent Magazine** has been a leader in gay parent resources since 1998.
    - www.gayparentmag.com

- **PFLAG National** is the largest organization for families, friends and allies united with people who are LGBTQ, working together to move equality forward.
    - www.pflag.org
    - Find your local chapter: www.pflag.org/findachapter
    - Email: info@pflag.org
    - Phone: (202) 467-8180

CPSIA information can be obtained
at www.ICGtesting.com
Printed in the USA
LVOW05s1055150716

496391LV00022B/148/P